THE IMPORTANCE OF AN AFRICAN-CENTERED EDUCATION FOR AFRICAN AMERICAN CHILDREN

BY: ROSALIE PEOPLES

ISBN: 978-1-957522-12-8
Published By: InspiredByVanessa
www.InspiredByVanessa.com

TABLE OF CONTENTS:

DEDICATION

I would like to dedicate this book to my friend Janine Bradford Lee and my sister Yolanda Peoples. For years I contemplated turning my writing project into a book. After speaking with Janine and expressing my idea, she encouraged me to move forward in this decision, leading to the day I created the dedication page. I would like to say Thanks my friend for your support and encouragement.

Yolanda, thank you for your support, encouragement, and willingness to assist me in any way you felt I needed to finalize this project.

To my Nephew Frank Bell, thank you for working so hard to create my book's cover. I presented you with an idea and your creative imagination took off.

I sincerely hope that everyone who reads this book takes the next step into digging further into their culture and making themselves the center of their education.

I would also like to give gratitude to my children: Eric Miles, Nathaniel, and Christopher, and grandchildren: Micheal, Malaysia, and Makye.

INTRODUCTION

"If you can control a man's thinking you do not have to concern yourself about what he will do. If you make a man feel that he is inferior, you do not have to compel him to accept an inferior status, for he will seek it himself. If you make a man think that he is justly an outcast, you do not have to order him to the back door. He will go without being told; And if there is not a back door, his very nature will demand one. Carter G. Woodson quotes"

Being in the education field for the past six years and having worked in predominantly European student/ faculty settings, I felt compelled to research the topic of the importance of an African-centered education. During my years of employment, I noticed that my African American students worked hard at trying to imitate their European counterparts. I found it disturbing that each year during Black History Month the same African Americans were discussed as if our history began and ended with Martin Luther King, Rosa Parks, Malcolm X, and George Washington Carver.

It became clear to me as I would engage in conversations with many African American children that they knew little or nothing about their history. I observed how they would cling to their white classmates and exclude other African American children when engaging in group activities. The African American children would try to imitate the dressing and speech styles of their white classmates. They seem to admire everything about their white counterparts. It seemed to me that the African American students were having an identity crisis. They were a minority in that particular town and in addition to this, they were not receiving any instruction in African American history (except instruction about a few selected African Americans). For these reasons, it became apparent to me that there is a need to incorporate African American history into African American children's education.

As a student in the inner city studies program, I have come to appreciate the important contributions made by African Americans as well as understanding that African American history goes beyond the few blacks who have gained achievements during the civil rights era. African American children should be made aware of the fact that African American history is not limited to slavery and its aftermath.

My research will attempt to provide the reader with the details about the importance of an African-centered education by looking at what scholars have said on the subject and what teachers, parents, and students said about African-centered education. The thought of educating Africans according to an African-centered viewpoint was introduced by Carter G. Woodson in his book The Miseducation of the Negro Race. The term miseducated was coined by Carter G Woodson. Woodson believed that many of the problems with the education of the Negro race were because the curriculum did not address the real social, economic, political, and cultural needs of black people. Woodson believed that if the miseducation continued it would eventually lead to the cultural death of the negro race. There are now many advocates who are fighting to establish African-centered institutions because they are concerned with the Eurocentric-centered curriculum presently being used throughout the public school system.

Woodson G. Carter. Mis-Education of the Negro (Trenton, NJ: African World Press, pg. 22, 25, 188.

CHAPTER 1:

THE IDENTITY CRISIS

During the 18th and 19th centuries, Western philosophers, such as Hegel, Hume, Montesquieu, and Gobineau, began a project of white supremacy that had been developed throughout the years and continues to be passed down to our youth. All of these Western philosophers believed and taught that the European race was the superior race and that Africans could not learn. They were barbarians, they did not contribute to world history, and some philosophers, like Hegel, removed Africans from history completely.

All of this misinformation has been presented to African Americans as well as white Americans and is the major reason that they need to be re-educated according to the African-centered educational views. By doing this the African American children will become aware that they are not a race without a history, and in fact, that they come from a very rich culture both spiritually and mentally. The misinformation that has been offered to our culture is a primary reason to reeducate our race using an African-centered approach.

There have been various definitions offered as to what is meant by education. Overall, an education should prepare a child to be able to effectively participate in society. The child should be able to think critically as well as analyze and resolve problems. An education should assist a person in having a feeling of assurance and confidence about themselves. The result of education should leave the person who has received the education feeling a sense of self-worth. While the European race is benefiting from the standard education being taught in public schools, the African-American child is lacking education in various areas. It has been argued that because the curriculum is European-centered African American students are not receiving an equal opportunity to learn about the role of African people in world history and therefore it is becoming difficult for them to progress educationally.

3 Carruthers H Jacob. Intellectual Warfare (Chicago: Third World Press, 1999), pg 6-7.

American schools serve as the cradle for miseducating minority children of various non-white ethnic groups. It is in these institutions that African American children first learn misinformation which eventually leads to them not having a positive image of themselves or their race. When African American children first entered the school system they began to form a positive concept of others and a negative concept of themselves. While in preschool and pre-kindergarten children are recited fairy tales, some of the most famous are; Cinderella, Jack and the Beanstalk, and Snow White. These fairy tales portray the Europeans as either being glamorous and beautiful or the hero at the end of the story. These stories usually begin by saying, it was a bright and beautiful day, or it was a dark and dreary day. The wicked person who is most often a wicked witch is wearing all black. These images of color assist the child at the start of their education to see black as ugly and bad and white as beautiful and nice.

As the child continues through school, they learn about European heroes such as Christopher Columbus, Abraham Lincoln, Thomas Jefferson, George Washington, and Marco Polo, to name a few. All of these individuals are presented to the African

American children as being heroic and/ or as well as enhancing America in some way. This is not to say that African Americans are not taught about but those that are taught about are repetitively and exclusively discussed throughout the K through 12 curriculums. Some of these individuals include Malcolm X, Martin Luther King, Rosa Parks, and George Washington Carver. While speaking to several African American children, I found that they all knew of these individuals and could recite something about them and their contributions to the African-American race, however, they could not name many others, and those that I named they knew nothing about.

I interviewed several children, parents, and educators both European and African American asking them various questions to get an understanding about how important it is to educate students using an African-centered approach, and how both parents and educators view the utilization of the method of education.

http://www.africawithin.com/carruthers/african-education.htm

CHAPTER 2:
INTERVIEWS

In this section, I present my findings based on several interviews that I conducted. Both of my interviewees who are administrators are African-American and they both are important stakeholders in the education of our students. I chose them precisely because of the vital role they play in running their respective institutions. As administrators, they are in charge of starting new initiatives and organizing and setting up committees to plan, design, and carry out the new initiative. So, for instance, in the case of designing an African-centered curriculum, it would be up to the administrators of the various schools to initiate the planning, designing, and implementing the new curriculum. Hence, I think that it is important to listen to what a few administrators have to say regarding this rather radical approach to the curriculum that I am proposing in this writing. I located these two individuals while doing an Internet search on the topic of African-centered curricula. I thought that both of these individuals might have interesting things to say about this topic and proceeded to contact them using the information that I obtained from their website.

TELEPHONE INTERVIEW WITH
MS. ROSEMARY MORIARTY

MILLER AFRICAN-CENTERED ACADEMY
PITTSBURG, PENNSYLVANIA
PRINCIPAL: MS. ROSEMARY MORIARTY
PHONE INTERVIEW
10:30 A.M.
4/7/2006

Before I started my interview officially, I asked Miss Moriarty if there was any information that she wanted to provide me with regarding the school. She said that Miller was the first and only African-centered public elementary school in Pittsburgh and Western Pennsylvania that emphasized a holistic approach focusing on administrative management strategies, staff development, curriculum reform, and parent and community involvement. The school's Afrocentric model requires a uniform dress code and infuses African and African American history and culture including knowledge, attitudes, and values into the core curricula. She advised me that Miller gave their proposal to the Board of Education to become an African center school in 1997. The school board accepted the proposal and developed a task force to see what African-centered education was all about. Dr. Asante, a scholar well versed in African-centered pedagogy, came to offer his support by providing the staff with the details about African-centered institutions. He also assisted in organizing them within the community.

The staff traveled from Pittsburgh to Detroit in 1997 and 1998 visiting several public schools that identified themselves as African-centered schools to help them to get a clearer understanding about how to run an African-centered school. Miller is at a public school and is required to follow the guidelines for all public schools.

The only difference is that in an African-centered curriculum, they are allowed to incorporate African culture-related studies into the curriculum.

My first question for Ms. Moriarty was for her to explain to me how her institution would define African-centered education. She said that an African-centered education is the placement of African American students at the center of the human process–in particular, the student is placed at the center of the educational experience. I then asked her if she would provide me with reasons why she believes that an African-centered education is more beneficial for African American children.

She said that the history of people of African descent has been distorted. False information has been presented to African American children for far too long. learning under an African-centered education will provide the students with the truth about the African race because for anyone to achieve greatness they must first learn to understand their own culture and history to love themselves.

I then questioned her about the student body. I wanted to know if there were students other than African Americans who attended the school and how they adapted to the African-centered approach. She said there were other races and she gave me the breakdown of the student body (see below). She also said that the other races were performing well and that an African-centered school is not just for African American children. She expressed the importance of other races understanding the truths about the African race. She states that African children have been exposed to the history of races other than their own for many years in traditional public schools.

The racial breakdown of the student body, according to Ms. Moriarty is as follows:

- African Americans: 97% of the student body
- Caucasians: 7% of the student body
- Asians: 7% of the student body
- Hispanics: 1.1% of the student body

I then asked her overall how the children were performing academically. She said that a person would have to do a serious study testing the children before attending and then during attendance, but many of the students have shown a greater improvement in test scores since they started attending Miller than before entering the school.

I asked her if she would provide me with some information about the curriculum. She said that in kindergarten, the children are taught about ancient Kemet, 2nd graders focus on Southern Africa, 3rd graders focus on Central Africa, 4th graders focus on Western Africa, and 5th graders study United States history. It is important that before studying the United States history the students know where the slave population originated.

TELEPHONE INTERVIEW WITH MRS. EFI MADGE WILLIS

MRS. MADGE WILLIS
DIRECTOR, NSOROMMA SCHOOL
4/13/2006
7:00 PM
ATLANTA, GEORGIA

I began my interview with Mrs. Willis by asking her to describe what the school's definition was of an African center education. She emailed me a form that the school issued to new parents explaining their definition of the meaning.

The term African-centric conjures up a wide range of images and emotions in people's minds. If frightens some, it surprises others, it confuses many, and it empowers those who understand it. In Mrs. Willis's own words, "We want to share with you an understanding of the term African-centered education that will hopefully give you strength, satisfy you, and let you know where we're coming from!"

African center education is a term used to describe many different types of school settings. Most educators use it to describe how they include information about people of African descent in the curriculum. Other schools teach African drumming and dancing and call that African-centered. The Council of independent black institutions (CIB) defines African-centered education in its 1994 position statement. (See www.cibi.org). Their definition emphasized the political aspect of self-determination as well as the teachers' conscious intent to learn about and become more African in their lives

According to Mrs. Willis at Nsoromma, when they say they are African-centered, they mean that their African heritage, the fact that they are people of African descent, is central to their understanding of who they are and what their situation is in the world. They mean that they use their heritage and culture to understand and analyze their history, to understand their present situation, and to plan for their future. It is not in opposition to anyone else's background nor against anyone else's plans, nor is it the only perspective that they should examine. It is about connecting with family first

I asked her why she believed that an African-centered education would be more beneficial for African American children. She responded that African-centered education is so important because it focuses on the needs of the students as well as responding to what is important to them.

I then asked her if there were races other than the African American race that attended the school and she said no, but they opened the door to anyone who wishes to attend. I asked her how the children perform academically compared to children attending traditional institutions. She responded:

"It varies, overall Nsoromma students are exposed to more information than most children and more than half of the students are performing at a grade level above where they are"

I asked her to provide me with information about the curriculum. She informed me that they developed their curriculum and exposed their students to the same subjects that are learned in other schools. The only difference is that in whatever they learn, an African theme is included. For example, in science, the students might be learning about air. The Lesson plan included air pollution, air animals, i.e. birds, air transportation, and air pressure, but along with learning this, they are taught about African American air travelers such as the Tuskegee Airmen. She said that this is the same with all the lessons; whatever they learn something related to Africa and Africans is always incorporated into the lesson.

Her next example was from social studies. The children learn that African people were not always slaves and they migrated into the world long before slavery. I asked her if she would agree or disagree that teaching according to African standard views teaches racism. During my research, many people opposed teaching this way claiming that in

In an African-centered curriculum, the children might learn to hate other races. She responded by saying "I would highly disagree. Racism can be defined in many different ways. Racism is usually carried out by people who have power because they can put their prejudice into action." She gave the example of an employer who refused to hire a person of a race that they didn't like or else hired them and placed them in the lowest-paying position. She ended by saying "I just would not agree with that because racism comes with power. What we do is help our children to get a comfortable feeling about themselves because when you love yourself you know how to love others. You have to know who you are and where you come from.

Receiving an African-center education is about family first."

I thanked Mrs. Willis for the interview and asked her if there was any other information she would like to share. She gave me their mission statement, explained to me how they came up with their institution's name and referred me to their website. The mission statement of the school is as follows:

"Our mission is to provide an excellent and comprehensive education in a nurturing and stimulating environment that emphasizes African culture. We seek to develop the whole child-the mental, physical, social and spiritual aspect, so the children can work towards creating a more humane existence not only for themselves, but for the entire world. In terms of education, African-centered education utilizes African and African American cultural perceptions, processes, laws and experiences to solve, guide, and understand human functioning relative to the educational process. African-center education is driven by truth, respect for knowledge, desire to learn, and a passion for excellence."

Dr. Noble:

The meaning of the name Nsoromma:

The star is one of the adinkra symbols from Ghana. It is translated as "Children of the sky!" or "Children of God." The school's children are regarded as stars with the potential to illuminate the universe as they develop their unique talents and gifts.

STUDENT INTERVIEW 1

ERIC HAMILTON (1989-2019)
DEKALB HIGH SCHOOL STUDENT
DEKALB, IL
10TH GRADE
MARCH 26, 2006
AFRICAN-AMERICAN
PERSONAL INTERVIEW

I asked Eric to tell me about African American people he has been taught about in school. The following is a summary of what he had to say:

The only time that black people have been taught about is during Black History Month. He learned about how Martin Luther King won the Nobel Peace Prize and did marches to protect against the racial mistreatment of blacks. He learned about how Rosa Parks conducted the Underground Railroad. He cannot remember much about Malcolm X, but he did learn about him in one of his classes. I then asked him if he felt that he has received more European history during school or African American history. Eric said that it was definitely more white history; In fact, he claimed that he was bored with studying so much European history.

I then asked Eric if he thought that if blacks were taught more African history, they would feel more positively about their race. Eric answered in the affirmative. He also said that when blacks are covered in the curricula, they are frequently portrayed negatively- this, he thought, was not going to help blacks develop racial confidence or pride. I then gave Eric a list of seven historically significant black individuals Benjamin Banneker, Sojourner Truth, Alexander Crummell, Booker T Washington, Ida B Wells, Barnett, Mary McLeod Bethune, and Charles Drew and I asked him if he had heard of any of them. He said that he had heard of Benjamin Banneker, Sojourner Truth, and Booker T Washington, but he could not tell me anything specific about them. The remaining names he had not even heard of.

At this moment I corrected Eric telling him that it was not Rosa Parks who conducted the Underground Railroad; it was Harriet Tubman. Once being corrected, he said "Oh, yes, I forgot it was Harriet Tubman. She was the girl that saved all of those slaves and there was some kind of song that they would sing to signal that they were about to leave." Rosa Parks was the lady who would not give up her seat on the bus.

STUDENT
INTERVIEW 2

JOHN HUGGINS
DEKALB HIGH SCHOOL STUDENT
DEKALB ILLINOIS
11TH GRADE
AFRICAN AMERICAN
MARCH 26, 2006
PERSONAL INTERVIEW

I asked John very nearly the same questions that I asked Eric. John said that he heard of Martin Luther King and Rosa Parks and he knew what their roles were during the Civil Right movement. He also said that he heard of a guy with "Big hair". I asked him if it was Frederick Douglass that he was referring to, and he said "Yes".

John also said that in school he was taught mostly white history. Very few blacks were talked about, (Martin Luther King and Rosa Parks were the most prominent). When I asked him if he knew about black history before slavery, he said that he knew a little about the Egyptians, though he was not sure if they were black or not.

I gave John the same list of prominent blacks that I had given Eric. John was able to identify Benjamin Banneker and Booker T Washington, but he said that he could not recall any details about these individuals.

STUDENT INTERVIEW 3

KEYVEANNA DORSEY
KRUSE
TINLEY PARK, ILLINOIS
3RD GRADE
AFRICAN-AMERICAN
MARCH 27, 2006
PERSONAL INTERVIEW

When interviewing Keyveanna, I did not ask her all the questions that I asked the others because of her young age. When asked about any blacks that she had learned about in school, she mentioned Martin Luther King. She said that she remembered him organizing boycotts and marches to protest against racism in society. She also said that she heard of Rosa Parks and the famous bus incident associated with her.

When asked if she learned more about white history or black history, without hesitation, she said that it was white history. When I gave the list of seven names to her, she said that she could not recognize any one of them. She did say that she would love to learn more about those individuals if her courses would cover them.

When I gave the list of seven names to Keyveanna, she said that she could not recognize any one of them. She did say that she would love to learn more about those individuals if her courses would cover them.

PARENT INTERVIEW 1

ANDRE H.
PARENT OF 1ST GRADER
BROWNELL SCHOOL
CHICAGO, ILLINOIS
APRIL 3, 2006
AFRICAN AMERICAN

I started the interview by asking Andre if knew what an African-centered education is. He said that it was learning about African government and politics. I then explained to him that an African-Centered education is an education that places the African American student at the center of the educational experience as a subject rather than an object. By placing the student at the center of the learning process, it allows for the inclusive process which gives equal representation of all races rather than one race over another.

After gaining a better understanding of what an African-centered education is, I then asked Andre if he would want his children to receive an African-centered education? He said that he would be interested in it;

however, he had no idea which school offered such a curriculum.

I then asked him if he believed that an African-centered education would help blacks have a more positive image of themselves. Andre said that he had no doubt that would be true. He said that he felt an African-centered education would also promote greater unity among people of African origin.

The last question that I put to him was if an African-Center education would promote racism among blacks. He disagreed with that notion and said that an African center curriculum would only promote racial pride and unity among the African American race.

PARENT
INTERVIEW 2

YOLANDA
PARENT OF 3RD GRADER
KRUSE SCHOOL
TINLEY PARK, ILLINOIS
MARCH 27TH, 2006
AFRICAN-AMERICAN

I asked Yolanda the same questions that I had asked Andre. Her responses were strikingly similar to the ones he had given me. Like Andre, Yolanda was not sure what an African-Center education was. Upon being explained, she readily agreed that it was an excellent idea; as it would enable the black race to feel proud about their racial heritage.

She said that her conversation with me made her curious as to how much African history was actually covered in her child's curricula since she was attending a school that has an African American student population of 7%. During this interview, she expressed that she was thinking about talking to the school's history teacher to get a better understanding as to why more African history was not covered

When I raised the question about the possibility of an African-centered education promoting racism against other races, she flatly denied it. She said that she believed that blacks were more forgiving people and learning more about their history is unlikely to make them behave in a racist manner towards others.

PERSONAL COMMENT

My interviews conducted with African American children substantiated my belief that African Americans should be educated using an African-centered approach. All of the interviewed children knew either little or nothing about their culture. They all stated that they learned more about European history than they did on their own.

INTERVIEW WITH NON-AFRICAN AMERICAN

BRITTANY
9TH GRADE STUDENT
HISPANIIC
CARL SANDBURG
TINLEY PARK, ILLINOIS
APRIL 8TH, 2006
PHONE INTERVIEW
7:15 P.M.

The questions that I asked Brittany were a little different from the questions that I asked the African American children. I began my interview by asking her to tell me about the different African American people that she learned about in school. She said that she knew about Harriet and how she developed the Underground Railroad. However, she admitted that she did not know a whole lot about other blacks simply because they were not covered in her curricula.

I asked her if she learned about blacks before slavery and Brittany said that she did not know anything about this topic. When asked what she knew about slavery, she said that she knew that blacks were forcibly brought into the country from Africa by whites. She said that she also knew that whites bought and sold blacks as if they were just another commodity.

I then asked her if she thought that her school taught more white history. She readily acknowledged that was true and she felt that if she had more black teachers, then maybe the emphasis would be different. I then asked her if she would be interested in learning more about black history. She said that she would be interested in learning more about black history and also all the injustices that whites had caused blacks throughout the centuries.

During my interview with those of non-African heritage, I discovered that their knowledge about African history was comparable to that of those that are African American. In Asante's article, "The Afrocentric Idea in Education", he advocates that children learn the true history of the African people. He not only believed that this was important for African Americans but also for other races, especially the European race because it would clarify their distorted beliefs about the African race. In my interview with Brittany, she expressed her beliefs about Africans and slavery. She said that the slaves were brought here to pick cotton and corn. She said that she learned that they were treated badly at times, but more often treatment was good. She said that they were clothed and fed well. What she does not know is that the jobs of the slaves extended beyond picking cotton and corn. She knew nothing about the torture and abuse that blacks endured from the slave owners. These are only a few of the areas about African history that should be made known.

INTERVIEW WITH
NON-AFRICAN AMERICAN (Teacher)

MS. C. K.
CAUCASIAN
INSTRUCTOR
CHICAGO PUBLIC SCHOOL (KINDERGARTEN)
CHICAGO, ILLINOIS
INTERVIEW VIA EMAIL
5/8/2006

The first question that I posed to her was if she knew what an African-centered education is. She said that an African-centered curriculum empowers black students by teaching them about black history and other related topics that will make the learning process meaningful to them. This, she added, will make them take an interest in their studies and as a result, turn them into active learners.

I then asked her if she believed that this type of curriculum would benefit black children. She said that she was convinced that such a curriculum would benefit them. She said that the existing curriculum was very racist in that it only focused on the achievements of the white race and slighted the achievements of other minority races. Having an African center curriculum would provide coverage of issues dealing with the history of the African people and it would make the curriculum much more appealing to black students. She emphasized the point that the fact that conventional history courses treat African history as a "Marginal" topic is extremely detrimental to young black children as it gives a rather negative image of the black race to.

I then asked her if she believed that implementing this type of curriculum would require that teachers be retrained. She said that she was sure that some retraining would be required and she, personally speaking, would be very enthusiastic about receiving such retraining. She describes such a retraining requirement as a process of professional growth and she said that this would indeed be needed for all teachers on a periodic basis.

The last question that I asked her was if she thought an African-Center curriculum would make black children racist. She vehemently rejected the idea, she said that this kind of curriculum would emphasize that any type of oppression is bad, therefore black children would not be in danger of becoming oppressors as a result of taking courses in such a curriculum. She ended by saying that such a minority center curriculum would teach students how terrible oppression (Of any type) is, and it will play a vital role in fighting existing societal oppression.

CONCLUSION

African American children are instructed to synthesize and memorize the ideas and belief systems of other races. They are conditioned to believe that all other races, especially the European race are superior to theirs. Truth needs to be restored to the teaching of African history, and this can begin by utilizing the African-Center approach to educating. African American children should see their race as being equally important to other races. They should understand that the African race did not begin during or around the time of slavery. For a person to understand themselves, they must first understand their history. It has to be acknowledged that the African race does have an important historical past that has contributed to shaping and forming this world which is why it should be covered in the curriculum.

ANNOTATED BIBLIOGRAPHY

Archie, Marlene.
Theories of Cultural Centeredness:
Multiculturalism and Realities.
Temple University

This article began with a very interesting story as well as an excellent example explaining why an African-centered education would be best for African American children. The story exemplifies the difference in language used by African Americans versus their European counterparts. The story ends by explaining that because of the difference in the way information is perceived a person would be considered to be lacking stability when the real problem is a misunderstanding between races. The term Centered Schools is used throughout the article and the definition given is "A school that places the student culture at the heart of the endeavor of education. A centered school centers its students culturally by way of beliefs that are fundamental to the idea of liberation through learning." It explains one reason for the development of a center school as being due to academic deterioration, declining enrollment, and low test scores. The article explains that by placing students at the center of what they are learning they become more engaged in the learning process, therefore creating an environment for better learning. The importance of multiculturalism as well as African-centered education is described and explained. Scholars with opposing views are also included in this article. The opposers are explaining why they are against educating outside of this traditional Eurocentric education that has been the main curriculum for education since the start of education.

This article is a very informative source for completing research on African-centered education. It offers much information on the subject, as well as opposing views. The ideas and views of various scholars are included in the article giving the reader a well-rounded scope of information.

Asante, Kete Moleif, The Afrocentric Idea in Education, Journal of Negro Education, Vol. 60. 1991

In this article, Asante examined the nature of the African-centered approach as well as established the need for it and suggested ways to develop it. The article gives descriptive reasons why school is attended. One reason given is to prepare a child to become part of a social group. Since almost all experiences in schools are based on Eurocentric history and are instructed from the standpoint of the white perspective, African children are almost forced to think as they do. It is explained that because of this, black children see themselves as an outsider and inferior to their race and because of this they should be instructed from an African-centered standpoint making sure that the African person and every situation, is centered around them. By doing this, the black child is not made to feel excluded from history, they see themselves as the subject or as participants of the education process. It is explained that when developing an African center curriculum it should include the story of the brutal treatment of blacks because African American children should be aware of the struggles of their ancestors. By informing them of this, the article is suggesting that it would probably enhance their behaviors and they will have a renewed sense of purpose and vision for their own lives.

Without this, misinformation will continually be exposed to our children and they will continue to see themselves as the problem. Asante feels an African-centered education will assist in strengthening the cultural identity of African children. The article concludes by saying that Afrocentricity provides all African Americans the opportunity to examine the perspectives of the African person and their contributions to the world history as well as their society and that the African center is not designed to be anti-white, but instead it is to help African American children to see that they are important to the human race.

This article is an excellent source of research on African-centered education. It gives details as to why this type of education is vital for African Americans, but it also will explain that it is not to teach racism in any way as many opposers to the African-centered education believe. A researcher can get useful information from this article. The article includes various information from different scholars who are experts on the subject of African-central education. It also contains many references that can be used in a bibliography for future research.

Carruthers, Jacob H "African-Centered Education."
http://www.africawithin.com/carruthers/african
_education.htm

In this article, Carruthers discussed the importance of instruction using an African-centered approach for African American children as well as offering several reasons why the African approach to education is best for African American children. The first reason is the philosophical views of the European children which is followed by the reasons for historical and cultural genocide against African people. He argues that using the African-centered approach would assist in clearing the falsification of the distorted images placed upon Africans and Africans. Thirdly, Carruthers expressed the need for Africans to develop their structure for restoring and maintaining their education. He expressed his reasons as being because Europeans have always had control politically, economically, socially, and educationally. A final reason given by Carruthers for being in favor of African center education is because he believes that only the cultural interests of the Europeans are being met. He feels that African American students are disconnected from the curriculum, and because of this, they are not receiving equality in education. He feels that since African

Americans live in predominantly African American communities and attend predominantly African American schools they should be taught from an African center perspective if they desire. This information was very useful in the understanding of the importance of African center education.

Giddings, Jahwara Geoffrey. "Infusion of Afrocentric Content Into The School Curriculum: Toward an Effective Movement." Journal of Black Studies, Vol. 31, 2001

This article examines the movement for an Afrocentric curriculum in Philadelphia's public schools and the reasons why it took place. During the 1960s community leaders and parents wanted more control over the school system. The schools that took on this curriculum were striving for five goals which were:

1. Developing necessary intellectual, moral, and emotional skills for accomplishing a productive, affirming life in society.
2. Providing an education structure that will rid itself of the negative images placed upon the Africans and their race replacing it with truth.

3. Including educational instruction that would use methods by their learning style.
4. Helping African American students to gather and maintain a positive self-concept.
5. Serve as a model for Blacks, transformation, and social action approaches to multicultural education.

While arguing why correctly presented African education is so important, the author gave an example using a textbook provided for school history use. The textbook stated that every black bought by slave traders was sold by one of his own race and that the slaves were better off than those who remained in bondage in Africa, as well as better off than many poor workers and peasants in Europe. The author refers to this as being appalling information.

The infusion of an Afrocentric view will serve as an attempt to reform the misinformation presented to African American children. The education system is described as being an institution of racism because of the views that it takes on. Reasons given to why the reform is so important is because of needing to alleviate the epidemic of low achievement, crime teenage pregnancy, and disrespect for self and elders.

Those in agreement with the reform strongly believe that if the reform fully takes place it will bring on many changes. The author supports these beliefs by arguing that through observation conducted, inquiries, and discussions it was found that students who were part of instruction that were centered around their own cultural information were better students, more disciplined, and had more motivation for school work.

Other authors were quoted who conducted their experiments with children taught from an African-centered viewpoint and found similar results. The article went into detail about the African-American Baseline Essay which was developed as a result of the Portland school districts need to provide a base of knowledge for teachers and it gives information on various other schools that have benefited from utilizing the essays. These essays are a collection of essays on art, language, math, science, and social studies and was designed by John Henrik Clark who was a scholar on African American studies.

This article is very useful for completing research on African-centered education. It gives information in various categories including why this type of education is needed for African Americans, the outcome it will have on students participating in an African center education, hands-on research such as interviews, and observations. It also includes information from many other scholars who are fighting for African center education. There are many references given that can be useful to compile a bibliography.

Haynes, M. Norris, <u>Critical Issues In Educating African American Children.</u> Maryland: IAAS Publishing Inc. 1993 pgs. 2-9

In this chapter, Haynes explains what he means by his ABCs of education. The ABCs of education are supposed to be a guide for educators who are educating African American children. This guide is supposed to make it easier for teachers to deal with the variety of African American children that they may come into contact with.

A. A is explained as being accepted. Acceptance by the author is explained as accepting all children regardless of their differences or learning styles.

B. B is explained as being belief, the author says that teachers have to change the way that they think about black youth because the way a person views someone affects how they react to their situation or needs.

C. C is explained as being challenged, the author explains that the results of not being accepted and having negative beliefs the expectations of the instructors are low and the students are not challenged. Haynes concludes by saying that by including African history into the curriculum of African American students it would enhance their interest therefore possibly stimulating and motivating the children to learn. The children would realize that Africans were a part of accomplishments and they offered many contributions.

This information was very interesting. The ABC method can be used with any curriculum or with any child who is performing at or below level. Although it did mention African history and methods for teaching African American children, I didn't feel this book was very useful in compiling research on African center education

Hillard, G Asa. And Luisa Martin. "The Education of African People: Contemporary Imperatives" http://www.nbufront.org/html/FRONTalView/ ArticlesPapers/asa1.html

In this article, the authors discuss the need for an African-centered education. They begin by making the reader aware that because African people do not know who they are, they are lost as a race and this places them in a life-and-death struggle. They assert that when Africans were first brought to the United States they knew who they were, but because Europeans realized how important the role of ethnicity plays in the success of cultures they have intentionally alienated Africans from their history. Hilliard insists that because false information has been passed down for centuries, it is being continued through the miseducation of African people. He strongly feels that the urgency is there to reestablish the African race. He also refers to Kotkin, the author of Tribes to assist in supporting his beliefs for the importance of races forming a strong identity. Hilliard mentions that Kotin refers to many classes except the Africans as being successful culturally. Among the classes mentioned were the Jews, Chinese, Japanese, Indians, and British. Kotin believes that although cultures possess a different history what makes them successful is when they share the following three critical characteristics.

1. "Strong ethnic identity and sense of mutual dependency that helps the group adjust to changes in the global, economic, and political order without losing its essential unity".

2. "A global network based on mutual trust that allows the tribe to function collectively beyond the confines or national or regional borders"

3. "A passion for technical and open-mindedness that fosters rapid culture and scientific development critical for success in the late 20th-century world economy". Africans are not seen as sharing these characteristics, as a result assisting in the breaking down of the race. The authors conclude by saying that before deciding on what to do about the education of African people, one must first accept the fact that Africans belong to an ethnic family and that they do have an important cultural past that should be exposed to our youth. It is explained that one way of exposing the cultural past of Africans can be achieved through designing a strong African-centered curriculum. Hilliard concludes by saying "For one to find himself, he

must first learn and know his heritage before learning others".

Khadija, J Jannah. <u>Improving the Motivation and Academic Achievement of African American Males:</u> An Observation of African Centered Education. Doctoral Dissertation. University of Houston. 1995

Jannah Khadija began her research by explaining the meaning of African-centered education. She explains it as being "Education that is multicultural with an emphasis on African and African culture. It is based on the belief that all humans have their physical, social, and intellectual origins and Africa. The child is placed at the center and through an exclusionary process, all representative groups are placed, not above or below any group, but alongside the rest of humanity." Her research shows that minority students of various ethnic backgrounds learn best in culturally compatible classrooms. An African-centered education creates an environment that makes the children feel that they are a part of the world and the educational experience whereas the traditional curriculum does just the opposite. This research gives historical information on an attempt to begin one of the earliest African-

American independent schools. Prince Hall, a veteran of the Revolutionary War, petitioned the city of Boston to establish a separate school for Africans due to the harassment being received by Africans in traditional schools. Although he was not successful in receiving help from Boston, he went on to start an alternative school in his son's home in 1798. Many others began to get involved realizing the need for improvement in the education of African American children. This led them to develop alternative approaches to teaching these children. This was the foundation for the African American independent education movement. The results of interviews conducted among various African American students are included in this research. These interviews were conducted to assist in understanding the best approaches to take when instructing African American children.

This research was very useful in completing research on African education. The interviews were most useful because they were first-hand information that showed results and proved many points on instructing African American children using the African center approach.

Lee, D. Carol. "Profile of an Independent Black Institution: African-Centered Education at Work." Journal of Negro Education, Vol. 61 No. 2. 1992

In this article, Lee describes what an African-centered institution should focus on. She also discussed one institution developed in Chicago. The New Concept Development Center of Chicago emerged from a group of black intellectuals who were associated with Third World Press which is an independent black publishing company. These individuals realized the need for African American children to be re-educated using an African-centered approach. The program began in 1972 as a Saturday program for African American children between the ages of 2-12. The goal of this program was to establish an educational institution within Chicago's Black community that would teach African American history and culture as well as teach the value of self-love. The article described what should be expected of an African center institution. The institution should:

1. "Legitimize African stores of knowledge."
2. "Positively exploit and scaffold productive community and cultural practices."
3. "Extend and build upon the indigenous language."

4. "Reinforce community ties and idolize the concept of service to one's family, community, and nation."
5. "Promote positive social relationships."
6. Impart a world view that idolizes a positive self-sufficient future for one's people without denying the self-worth and right to self-determination of others."
7. "Support cultural continuity while promoting critical consciousness."
8. "Promote the vision of individuals and communities as producers rather than a simple consumer."

The "Nguzo Saba" style is important to the African-centered educational movement. The article includes what the Nguzo Saba Style is: Nguzo Saba is the Black Values System, which is a system of seven principles:

1. Umoja-unity
2. Kujichagulia-self-determination
3. Ujima-collective work and responsibility
4. Ujamaa-Cooperative economics
5. Kuumba-creativity
6. Nia-purpose
7. Imani-faith.

Lee explains that both parents and teachers participating in an African-centered institution are expected to be committed to the beliefs of what an African-centered institute stands for.

The information in the article was extremely useful to someone researching the topic of African-centered education. It gives precise details of what the institution is based on as well as what is expected of everyone willing to be involved in an African-centered institution.

Madhubuti, Hakiand and Safisha Madhubuti. <u>African-Centered Education: Its Value Importance, and Necessity In the Development of Black Children. Chicago:</u> Third World Press, 1994

These two authors reiterated the information that Carol Lee's article contained. They discussed the need for an African center education and gave details concerning why it is vital for educating African American children. The expectation of an African center education is discussed and it is similar to the information given in Lee's article. The need for an African-centered pedagogy is given. This section states that because racism is still a large existing problem and

Europeans still think of themselves as superior, the need for African American children to realize that they are equally a part of the human race is a serious issue. The public education system is based on European-centered views and as long as this continues African American children will never see themselves as being anything other than victims according to the article. The author stressed and supported their findings for an African-centered education. One of their supporting beliefs is that this type of education will possibly contribute to achieving pride, equity, power, wealth, and cultural continuity for African Americans and for building ethical character among the African community. The chapter concludes by saying that if Africans develop a strong cultural sense of self and a commitment and connection with their race it will help them to rise as a race. Both of these authors are involved with the New Concept Development Center which is an alternative school for African American children that began as a Saturday program in 1972 and is still in full force today.

This chapter contains useful information for the research of African-centered education. It reiterates much of what Carol Lee's article on Profile of an Independent Black Institution; African-Centered

Education At Work stated. Their views were the same on what is to be expected of an African-centered institution. This book went a step further by giving important details on why an African-centered pedagogy is vital for the African-American race.

Porter, Michael. <u>Kill Them Before They Grow: Misdiagnosis of African American Boys In American Classrooms.</u> Chicago: African American Images, 1997

In this book, Porter argues that an African-centered education is important. He provides the reader with examples of studies conducted among students being taught from an African-centered perspective. The reasons he gives are an argument with Haki Madhubuti & Safisha Madhubuti. Porter feels that because public schools are controlled by the European power and because of the high degree of racism Africans need to create an educational curriculum that relates specifically to their race where they can learn specifically about the accomplishments of their own culture instead of the Europeans. Details are given on how to distinguish between Africans who suffer from pathology. The author's definition of this is a black person who is in disagreement with anything that is associated with being African-centered. The book says that when blacks are suffering with this, they have no problem relating to what is said to be factual according to Europeans; Examples given are a white Santa Claus, White fairies, and a White Christ. The miseducation of his group of people is given as the reason for their pathology. Individuals suffering from this view their races as being inferior to other races.

An example of studies on African American children and their attitude towards the change in the curriculum was included in this book. In one study conducted African American children who were taught about their ancestors dating as far back as 4100 B.C. showed an elevated degree of interest and participated in discussions during class. Children relating themselves to a discussion assisted in the changing of both attitude and behavior. The difference in opinion of Europeans relating to African-centered education was given and explained as being a disagreement with this type of education out of fear. The book concludes by saying that white children are aware of their race and are taught that the world belongs to them while black children are being miseducated to see themselves as an inferior race. It goes on to offer the importance of coming together as a race. Porter states that for Africans to move forward it must be understood that African-centered, African-operated, and African-owned is best for Africans and this especially holds with the educational system.

The information offered in this book will assist in research on the topic of African-centered education. The author gives reasons supported by hands-on research. He gives a meaning as to why Africans see themselves as inferior, as well as details on ways of correcting the problem.

Woodson, G. Carter. <u>The Miseducation of the Negro</u>. African World Press, 1990

Woodson explains fundamental problems in the education of African American people. It is explained that African Americans have been wrongly educated. They have been educated to detach themselves from their own culture and to attach themselves to the European culture. The education received by Africans from Europeans is described as the enslavement of the mind. He explains that because of this, the African culture is facing psychological, as well as, cultural death because the information being received about their race is distorted and many facts have been omitted. Historical information is offered explaining how the miseducation of the African-American race began. Blacks were not intended to have a formal education, but instead to be educated for a trade, such as cooking, or cleaning. When they did begin to receive formal education they were taught from the perspective of the Europeans, therefore leading to the spreading of incorrect information about Africans and the African culture. Information is offered about Africans who were taught to view Europeans and the Eurocentric culture as superior. These Africans became so engaged with the information received from (who were considered) scholars, that they began to see themselves as inferior, and believed that by detaching themselves from their race they could change who they were. The point stresses that to strengthen the African American race they will have to forget what was told and passed on by the Europeans and be re-educated with correct information. Woodson's book on miseducation was the gateway for beginning the movement to reform the education being offered to African American students.

This is a very useful source for research on African-centered education. It gives not only historical information that is useful for understanding why the movement is necessary, but it also gives information as to why and how the miseducation of the Africans began. It offers information concerning why and how information needs to be achieved to reverse the process of African education in an effort for them to become culturally aware of their race.

OPPOSING VIEWS TO AFRICAN-CENTERED EDUCATION

Famularo, J. Thomas. Education Opposing View-
points: <u>Multicultural Education Is Counter-</u>
<u>productive</u>. San Diego, California: Greenhaven
Press, 2000 pgs. 103-108

In this chapter, the author argues the point that
centering education based on students' culture is not
beneficial. The chapter explains that educating
students centered around their education will result
in declining educational qualities, and it is also a
"Shallow and superficial way to educate." It states
that education should remain traditional, covering
Eurocentric history because not educating using this
technique will deny the existence of a common
American culture. Details are given offering many
other reasons why educating students centered

around their culture is nonproductive. Some of the reasons mentioned are:

1. All students should share a common body of knowledge after completing school and a centered-based education will not allow for this to happen therefore leaving students outside of the European race ignorant.

2. A centered-based education is described as being a danger because it will teach hatred and racism towards other races.

3. Lastly, an education based on culture is nonproductive because the overseer of the curriculum design is to teach information that will not equip the students with the information they would need to continue throughout life.

This source is beneficial for an imposing view on African-centered education. It gives various details stating why this type of education is not productive for students. The author refers to other scholars who agree with his idea. This book offers views of both those who agree with and those who oppose African-centered education.

Schlesinger, M. Arthur Jr. The Disuniting of America. New York London: W.W. Norton & Company, 1991 pgs. 79-124

In this chapter, Schlesinger is attacking the thought of multicultural education by saying that children should not be taught according to their cultures. He specifically mentions Afrocentric studies saying that people go along with the thought of Afrocentric education due to the hardship blacks endured during slavery. It is stated that a centered education is none other than a self-interested group. The fact is stress that teaching a centered-based education is useless no matter what race it is. It is believed that all children should be taught using the traditional Eurocentric approach. When this is not achieved it is insinuated that it replaces integration with separatism. America is described as being a melting pot according to the author and when teaching is based on any specific culture it is the doorway to racism and hatred among racists as well as

disuniting America as a whole. Overall Schlesinger is saying that by specifically focusing on African Studies with African American students it is a way to support mythical claims and try to convince the participants of this type of study false beliefs about history. One example used to support his idea of a false belief is that Africa was the birthplace of science, religion, philosophy, and technology. Another example given by the author of a false belief that has been passed down throughout African American history is the story of Charles R Drew, the inventor of blood plasma storage. According to the story Drew was denied treatment at the hospital he was taken to because he was black and at a white hospital. The author insists that this story is not true. Drew was seen by the doctors at this hospital and died during surgery. It is asserted by the author that support of African-centered studies believes that re-educating the children will assist in bringing up their self-esteem, but he feels that it does the exact opposite, setting the children up for failure instead. The European ideas and beliefs are upheld by him and the point is stressed that this is the best method to use as a curriculum.

In this book, Schlesinger makes many very convincing points. He strongly believes that the information offered by African American scholars is false and a hazard to not only the African race but the American Race as a whole. He gives quotes from many other scholars who are in support of the Western Cultural curriculum. This is an excellent source for opposing views on the subject of African-centered education.

Watkin, William H. The White Architects of Black Education: Ideology and Power in America 1865-1954. New York: Teachers College Press, 2001 pg. 43-61

This particular chapter discusses Samuel Chapman Armstrong, the founder of Hampton Institute in Virginia. Armstrong described his beliefs of the superiority of Europeans over Africans. It is explained that Africans do have the ability to learn and become civilized but compared them to creatures of the wild that had to be tamed. Deficiency of character is explained as being the primary problem for Africans. The chapter concludes by saying that educating Africans in the area of industrialism was best for them. Hampton's theory on educating Africans influenced the way blacks were educated for 100 years.

The information given is useful. It provides historical information assisting in understanding why Europeans are in disagreement with an African-centered education as well as why this is such a debated issue. This chapter will assist in understanding some of the negative images placed on the African race. Some of the negative information given about Africans and Africa will help the reader understand why it is necessary to reeducate children using the African-centered approach.

ABOUT THE AUTHOR

Rosalie Peoples, author of The Importance of an African-Centered Education for African American Children." She was born and raised in Chicago, Illinois. She is the mother of four children (Eric 1988-2019) Miles, Nathaniel, Christopher. She received her M.A. in Inner City Studies from Northeastern, Il University School of Education. Her studies of the education system while pursuing her M.A. resulted in her writing her first book.

Rosalie is affiliated with several organizations, including:

- Who's Who Among American College Students
- Phi Theta Kappa Honors Society
- Who's Who of Professional Women

Rosalie has completed and presented several research presentations including:

- The History of Rum and the Ties the Barcardi Family had with slavery
- Institutional Slavery, The Prison System and Minorities
- The Barclay Brothers Business of Banking and Slavery

www.ingramcontent.com/pod-product-compliance
Lightning Source LLC
Chambersburg PA
CBHW071239090426
42736CB00014B/3141